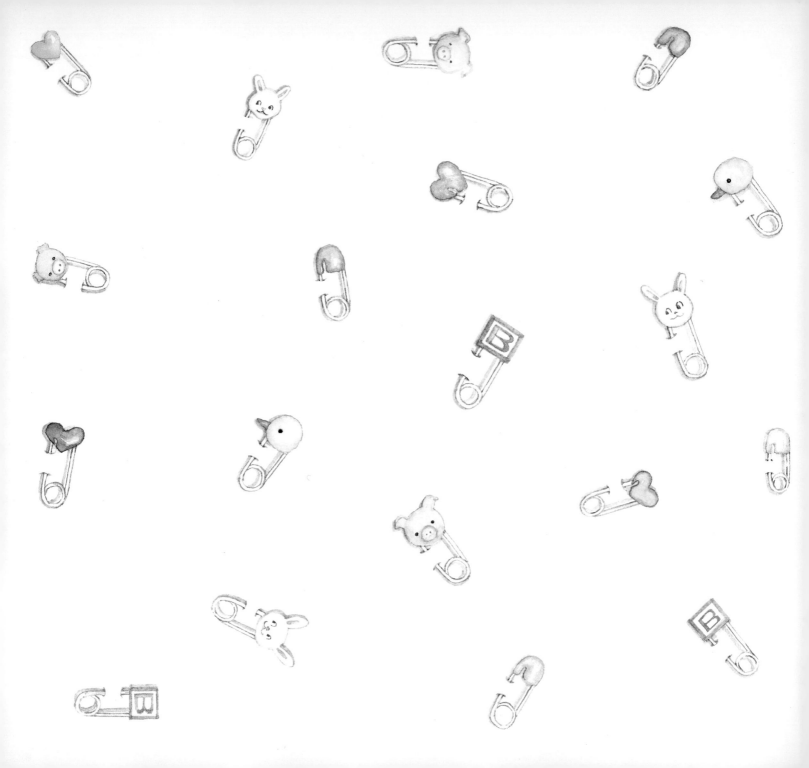

BABY LOVE

BY
SUSAN BRANCH

CUT OUT A
LITTLE PICTURE
OF BABY'S FACE
& GLUE IT HERE.

This book
belongs to

A KEEPSAKE BOOK FROM
THE HEART OF THE HOME

Little, Brown & Company
Boston Toronto London

FIRST EDITION

ISBN 0-316-10639-9

10   9   8   7   6   5

Published simultaneously in Canada by Little, Brown & Company (Canada) Limited

PRINTED IN HONG KONG

Here's to the little,
to the tiny,
to the small;
To the ones that aren't big,
And to those that aren't tall. ♡

glue here, a
picture of the
Father-to-be

"Last thing I remember I was living all alone—
No one on my front porch; no one on the phone.
Miracles can happen—one did when I found you
And now all of a sudden, the miracles are two."

Charles R. Stewart

and here,
the
Mother-
to-
be.

A LADY-IN-WAITING
(I'm pregnant!)

I first found out: _____

My feelings & thoughts: _____
_____
_____
_____

Baby's due date: _____

Who I told: _____

What'd they say: _____
_____

Private Celebrations: _____
_____

Plans: _____
_____

My full name & age: _____

. . . AND WAITING

Father-to-be says: _____

_____ His full name & age: _____

First shopping trip for baby: _____

_____

_____

_____

_____

_____ Who spoils me? _____

_____

_____

_____

_____

Pickles & Ice Cream – Favorite Foods: _____

_____

_____ Favorite Outfits: _____

_____

_____

♪ a walking illustration of his adoration ♥ His love makes me beautiful, so beautiful, just BEAUTIFUL... ♪ I am the beautiful reflection of my love's affection,

glue photo here

MOM BLOOMS
date : _____

N E W   L I F E

I FELT THE BABY MOVE: _____

How the baby moves — & moves ME:

Doctor Visits:

_____

_____

_____

_____

_____

Special Medical Stuff, Classes?

_____

_____

_____

_____

_____

Diary

"Such solicitous care I have never had. Chairs pulled out for me, things picked up for me, milk offered me, an arm offered for high steps.... At first it bothered me; now I think it rather a relief—sometimes very funny and sometimes very nice."

♥ Anne Morrow Lindbergh

CHOOSING THE NAME

And while we're waiting...

THE HISTORY OF MOM & DAD

_____

_____

_____

_____

_____

_____

_____

_____

_____

_____

_____

_____

❀ HOW WE MET · OUR JOBS · SCHOOLS · CHILDHOODS ❀

The water is wide, I cannot cross o'er.

Neither have I the wings to fly.

And both shall row, my love and I.

Build me a boat that can carry two,

Baby Shower

FRIENDS FUN FOOD GIFTS

A Star Is Born

Baby's Full Name _____

Named For _____

Birthday _____

Day of the Week _____ Time _____

Place _____

Who was There _____

Baby's Weight _____ Length _____

Any Hair? _____ Color _____

Skin Color _____ Eye Color _____

Baby Looks Like _____

STAR LIGHT, STAR BRIGHT, I HAVE A BABY. GOOD NIGHT.

FIRST PHOTO

The picture of perfection . . .

The night before •
Labor & birth •
First sighting •
Mirades •
Mewing &
cooing •
How's
Dad •
?

OUR FAVORITE  CARDs & NOTES

Special Cards & Notes

First Visitors

"Little boats should keep near shore."

Benjamin Franklin

BABY ANNOUNCEMENT

we have our
B U N D L E   O F   J O Y

NEWSPAPER

ANNOUNCEMENT

picture of
Baby's
face

Hello Love

BABY'S

glue
photo
here

FIRST HOME

Address_____
Phone Number_____

WELCOME HOME

Special preparations · Where baby
eats, sleeps & plays · Who visits
most often · What the house is like ·

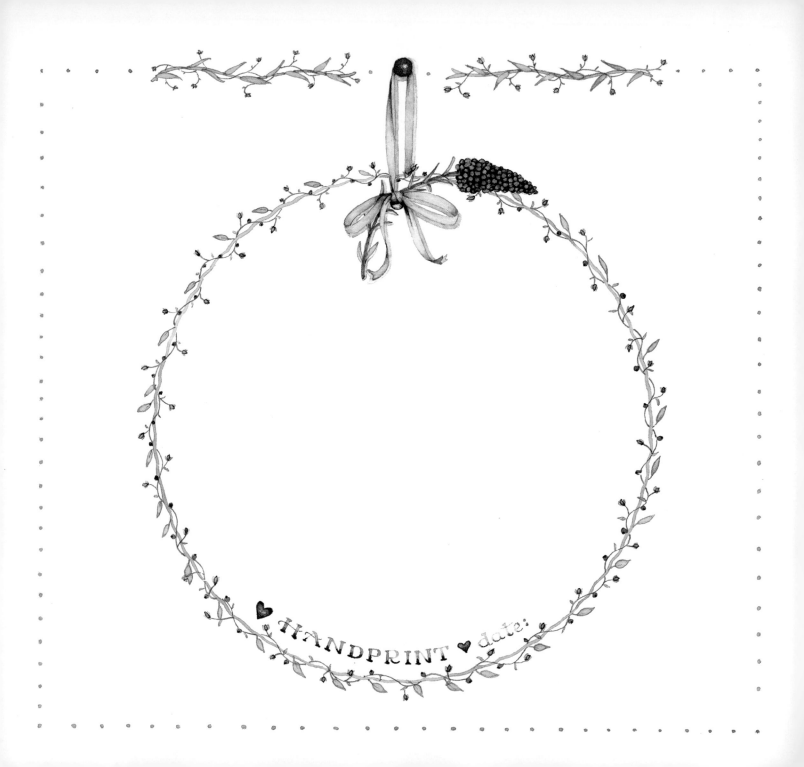

HANDPRINT ♥ date:

FOOTPRINT ♥ date:

Put your little tootsie here, dear ♥.

FIRST WEEKS

in

B A B Y L A N D

"I actually remember feeling delight, at two o'clock in the morning, when the baby woke for his feed, because I so longed to have another look at him."

♥ Margaret Drabble

FIRST WEEKS

The Family · Some History

Brothers · Sisters · Aunts · Uncles · Cousins · Nieces · Nephews

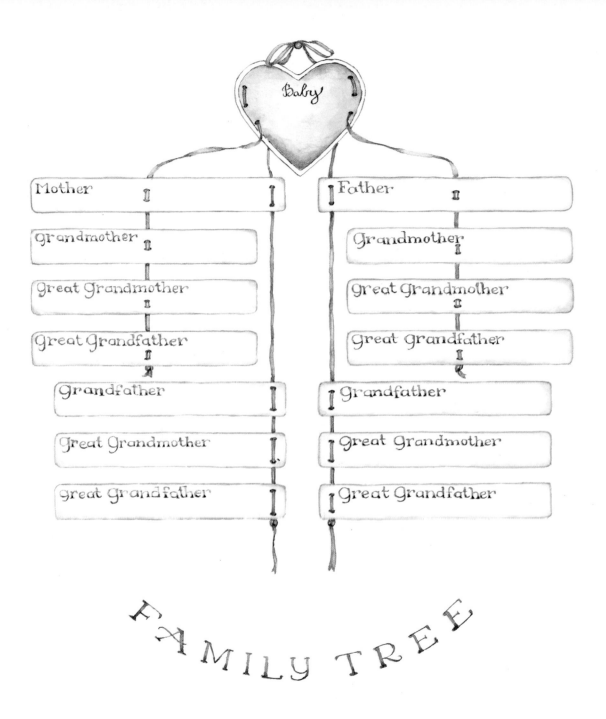

Baby

Mother

Father

Grandmother

Grandmother

Great Grandmother

Great Grandmother

Great Grandfather

Great Grandfather

Grandfather

Grandfather

Great Grandmother

Great Grandmother

Great Grandfather

Great Grandfather

FAMILY TREE

SPIRITUAL & RELIGIOUS
CEREMONIES & CELEBRATIONS

Baby's
FIRST OUTINGS

WHAT WE DO · WHERE WE GO · WHO WE SEE

ASTROLOGICALLY SPEAKING

Baby's sign & what it means: _____

Birthstone _____

Flower _____

A Sign of the Times

trends · fashions · news · music

what's going on?

STICK
POSTAGE STAMP
HERE

politics · sports · movies

BABY'S SCHEDULE

feeding, baths, napping, bedtime

_____

_____

_____

_____

_____

_____

_____

_____

_____

_____

BABY'S FOOD

Nursing
Bottles
Solid Food
Weaning
Likes &
Dislikes

In my bed, while I was sleeping,

Glue a tiny
envelope
here

Mom cut off a lock of hair—

So when I'm grown I'll find it there.

Between these pages she has laid it,

date:_____

BABY SLEEPS

SWEET DREAMS

BABY'S FIRST CLOTHES
soft, snuggly, and sweet

You can save a favorite outfit & have it framed, complete with socks or booties, ribbons or hats — add a picture of baby IN the outfit ♥

BABY GETS DRESSED

BATH TIME

God loveth the clean.

Paste Embarrassing Picture Here

O. U. Q. T.!

BABY'S GROWTH

Age	Weight lbs.	ozs.	Height ft.	ins.
one week				
two weeks				
one month				
two months				
three months				
four months				
five months				
six months				
seven months				
eight months				
nine months				
ten months				
eleven months				
one year				
two years				
three years				
four years				
five years				

Notes

MAKING MEMORIES

♥♥♥ When your baby is 4 or 5 months old, invite all the women from your birthing classes to a Baby Party at your house. Prop the babies up on the couch, all in a row, wearing only their diapers & take pictures of them. These little fat cuties who can't quite sit up & barely focus, make the best picture you can imagine — add a few balloons to the photo. Of course, later on, this will be proof that your baby was the CUTEST OF ALL!

♥♥♥ I saw this idea in a magazine — in the 1940's a man bought a stylish grown-up bathing suit for his brand new baby daughter. He began photographing her in it every year until she finally grew into it. It made a funny, charming, & loving record of her growth. ♥

♥♥♥ Ask your Grandma to talk about her childhood. Have her describe holidays, Sundays, school, vacations, her parents' home, her siblings. Tape these memories & save them for your children. ♥

START A HOPE CHEST

You can use an old toy box, a steamer trunk, or even a sturdy box — it doesn't matter, it's the stuff *inside* that counts ♥
Some ideas:

Great Grandma's hand embroidered dish towels

Baby's books

Scrapbook

Each year: a sterling silver place setting

To drink on "Baby's" Wedding Day

FINE WINE

HOME SWEET

An old quilt

favorite bear

SUGAR COOKIES

Aunt Mary's famous Sugar Cookie recipe

Letters, photos, keepsakes

A cute outfit

F O R   B O Y S   A N D   G I R L S

" Wherever I am,
                there's always Pooh,
        There's always Pooh and Me.
   Whatever I do, he wants to do,
        " Where are you going to-day?'
                    says Pooh :
   'Well, that's very odd 'cos I was too.
   Let's go together,' says Pooh, says he.
        'Let's go together,' says Pooh . "

                A. A. Milne

First Evening Out Without Baby

SWEETPEA

KISSES GOODNIGHT

Magic Moments

Dates

When you first:

Slept through the night: _____

Smiled: _____

Laughed out loud: _____

Turned over: _____

Sat up alone: _____

Crawled: _____

Stood alone: _____

Got a tooth: _____

Spoke 1st word: _____

Walked, took steps: _____

When you first:

Drank from a cup: _____ BABY

Used a spoon: _____

Danced: _____

Blew out a candle: _____

Ate dirt (or other special treats): _____

Ran: _____

Said "Mommy" & "Daddy": _____

Played a joke: _____

Waved "Bye-Bye": _____

★ what a smart baby! ★

SWEET REFLECTIONS

SWEET REFLECTIONS

Cleaning & scrubbing can wait till tomorrow,
For babies grow up, we've learned to our sorrow;
So quiet down, cobwebs,
Dust, go to sleep!
I'm rocking my baby, & babies don't keep.

Photo

Babies don't keep. ♥

A GAME TO PLAY ON BABY'S FEET

Gently slap the bottom of baby's bare foot
& in a sing-song voice, say:

" Shoe a little horse, shoe a little mare,
but let the little baby go bare-bare-bare. "

BABY'S HEALTH RECORD

Visits to Doctor

I do not like thee, Doctor Fell,
The reason why I cannot tell;
But this I know, and know full well,
I do not like thee, Doctor Fell.

~ Mother Goose

T E E T H I N G

First tooth appears: _____

upper

Baby's Teeth

lower

GAMES TO PLAY ON BABIES' FACES

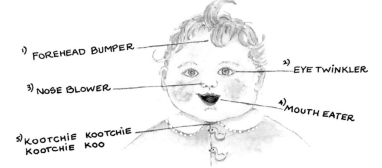

1) FOREHEAD BUMPER

2) EYE TWINKLER

3) NOSE BLOWER

4) MOUTH EATER

5) KOOTCHIE KOOTCHIE KOOTCHIE KOO

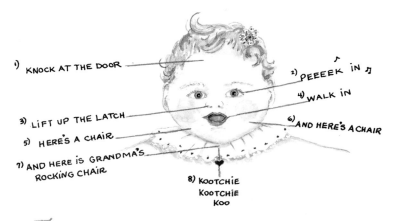

1) KNOCK AT THE DOOR

2) PEEEEK IN ♪♫

3) LIFT UP THE LATCH

4) WALK IN

5) HERE'S A CHAIR

6) AND HERE'S A CHAIR

7) AND HERE IS GRANDMA'S ROCKING CHAIR

8) KOOTCHIE KOOTCHIE KOO

Touch your fingers to your baby's forehead, eyes, nose, mouth & cheeks ~ tickle under the chin ♥.

BABY FEARS

can cause tears
~ poor baby ~

Birds · Dreams · Thunder · Toys ·

Ocean Waves · Dogs · Loud Noises · Bugs

· Funny Faces · Water · Fireworks ·

T E N D E R · M O M E N T S

SAY "I" + POINT TO YOUR EYE; AND "LOVE" + PAT YOUR HEART; AND "YOU!" + POINT TO YOUR BABY. HE'LL LEARN THIS TOO AFTER A WHILE.

IF YOU HAVE TO GO TO WORK YOU CAN VIDEO YOURSELVES TELLING YOUR CHILD HOW MUCH YOU LOVE HIM — SING FOR HIM & THEN HE WILL "HAVE" YOU WHILE YOU'RE GONE.

AS BABY GROWS UP, SET ASIDE A SPECIAL DAY APPROX. 6 MO. AFTER HIS B'DAY. CALL IT "JOEY'S DAY" (FOR EXAMPLE) A HAPPY UN-BIRTHDAY!"

HAVE EYE CONTACT — WATCH YOUR BABY + WHEN HIS GLANCE LIGHTS ON A SPECIAL OBJECT, TAKE HIM TO IT — SHOW IT TO HIM.

Baby

Love

KISS BABY'S OPEN HAND & THEN ROLL IT CLOSED SO HE CAN SAVE IT.

MOM + DAD MAKE A "BABY SANDWICH" — THEY HUG EACH OTHER WITH BABY IN THE MIDDLE. WITH MORE CHILDREN DO A "FAMILY HUDDLE" — EXCHANGE KISSES.

LET YOUR CHILD SNUGGLE INTO BED WITH YOU.

THE MOST IMPORTANT WAY TO SHOW LOVE IS WITH YOUR TIME.

STORYBOOKS

Tried & true, your baby will love these "first" books. ♥

Goodnight Moon by Margaret Wise Brown
The Runaway Bunny by Margaret Wise Brown
The Baby's Catalogue by Janet & Allan Ahlberg
Peek A Boo by Janet & Allan Ahlberg
Andrew's Bath by David McPhail
First Things First by Charlotte Voake
Pat the Bunny by Dorothy Kunhardt
The Very Busy Spider by Eric Carle
Richard Scarry's Busy Busy World
Helen Oxenbury's Board Books: Dressing, Family, Friends, Playing, Working

OUR FAVORITES

Adventures in Self Expression

what a baby!

BABY CLAPPED! _____

_____ and plays Patty Cake _____

Baby can Meow, Moo, & Baaa! _____

_____

Baby Plays Peek-a-Boo! _____

_____ hides & seeks _____

_____

♪ Baby Sings ♪ _____

_____

BABY'S 1ST MUSICAL INSTRUMENT _____

_____

Baby Dresses Up _____

_____

BUDDING ARTIST
Baby Starts to Draw

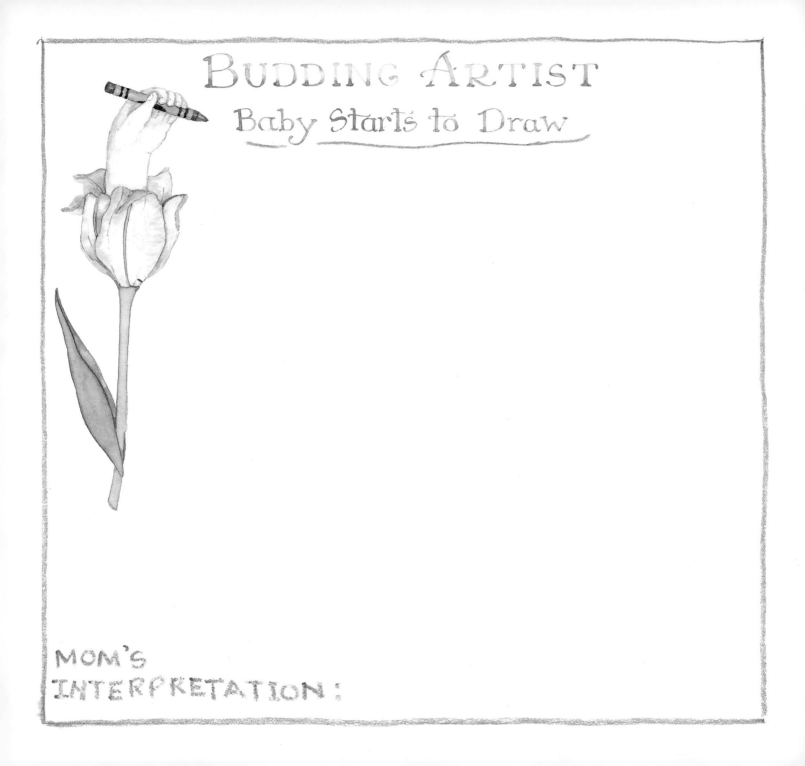

MOM'S
INTERPRETATION:

Give your baby his own star. Look into the night sky together and show him just which one is his. Tell him it's there to watch over him and for him to make wishes on.

Take baby on a tour of house and garden — show him things: grass, flowers, birds, clouds, airplanes, and colorful objects in the house — stop at all the mirrors and dance.

Put a bird feeder outside baby's window where he can see it from his bed.

Talk to the baby constantly as you work around the house — tell him what you're doing.

Tie bells on the baby's shoes.

The nicest thing you can do for your child (and yourself!) is to read to him every day.

Hug a tree — show baby respect for the earth. Lie in the warm grass and watch the clouds float by as you tell him about nature's magic. Watch the sunset together.

When appealing to your baby (and everybody else!) think about the five senses. Excite his sense of touch, sight, hearing, taste and smell.

BABY TALK

FAVORITES
toys, books, friends, foods

"A child of one can be taught not to do certain things such as touch a hot stove, turn on the gas, pull lamps off their tables by their cords, Or wake mommy before noon."

Joan Rivers

MOTHER NATURE

Weather

Seasons

Animals

Gardens

EARTH LOVE

VARIATIONS ON THE PIGGY POEM

Wiggle baby's toes, starting with the "big" one, as you say each line.

The Original Piggy Poem:

This little piggy went to market,
This little piggy stayed home.
This little piggy had roast beef,
This little piggy had none.
And <u>this</u> little piggy went wee-wee-
wee-wee all the way home.

For the vegetarian child change line 3 to:
This little piggy had bean soup.

For the "hip" child change last line to:
But this little piggy was a Boogie Woogie piggy
& he Boogie Woogied all the way home.

BABY SHOWS LOVE

Mom's first real hug & first real kiss:

FUNNY STUFF

You were sooooo funny!

VACATIONS

MOTHER'S LITTLE HELPER

HOW WE SURVIVED
THE TERRIBLE TWOS

"Fortunately for children, the uncertainties of the present always give way to the enchanted possibilities of the future."

— Gelsey Kirkland

BABY LEARNS

Knows colors, can count, ties shoes, etc.

Becoming Civilized

Eating at the table; the "magic words": please & thank you; sharing & caring

TAKE YOUR BABY TO FAST FOOD PLACES TO PRACTICE EATING IN RESTAURANTS

HOLIDAY CELEBRATIONS

A picture of baby's face

First Year

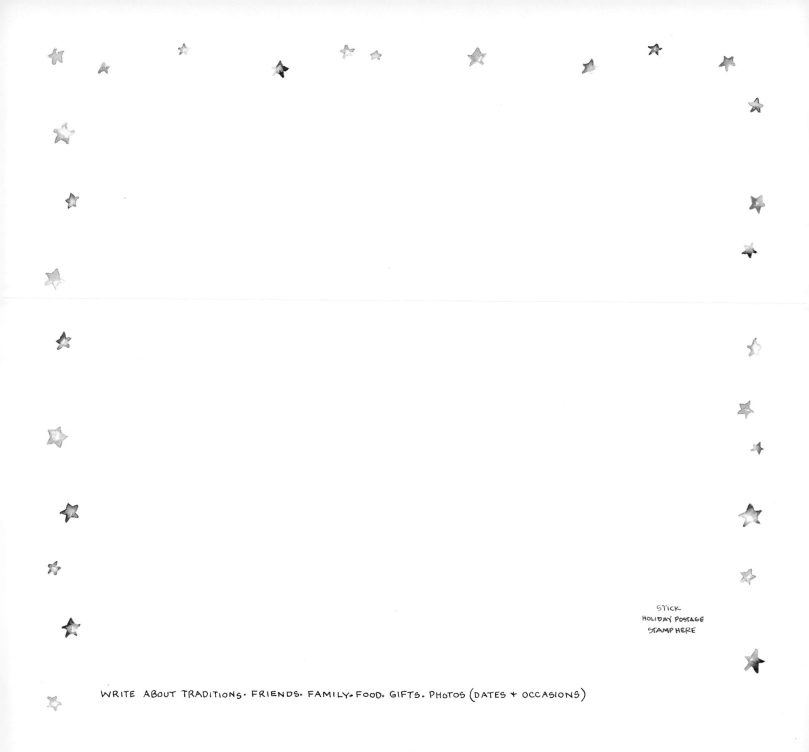

STICK
HOLIDAY POSTAGE
STAMP HERE

WRITE ABOUT TRADITIONS. FRIENDS. FAMILY. FOOD. GIFTS. PHOTOS (DATES + OCCASIONS)

HOLIDAY CELEBRATIONS

2nd Year

Baby's Face

Stick
Postage
Stamp
here

glue photo
here

glue photo
here

BABY CELEBRATES

Holiday Celebrations

_____

_____

_____

_____

_____

_____

_____

_____

_____

_____

_____

_____

Baby's
Face ♥

THIRD · · · · · YEAR

Glue photo here

Stick
Postage
Stamp
here

Glue photo here

TRICK OR TREAT!

Paste picture
here ♡

Boo!

Valentine's Day

B A B Y

BABY'S
PICTURE

K I S S E S

Kiss

Kiss

You can leave a sweet imprint here by putting lipstick on your child and having him kiss the page.
(This also makes a very nice Valentine from you and baby to daddy.)

· FIRST BIRTHDAY ·

· BABY CAKES ·

A picture is worth a thousand words

BIRTHDAYS

2

3

ABC's and 123's

SCHOOL DAYS

"All that I am or hope to be,
I owe to my angel mother."

Abraham Lincoln

• BABY SIGNS NAME •

Mom talks about her life —work, love, friends, motherhood. . . .

Mother says

FAMOUS LAST WORDS

If you don't stop, your face will freeze like that. I only have two hands. Let me kiss it and make it better. Because I said so. Because I'm the mommy, that's why. Go ask your father. Wear clean under-wear — you could get in an accident. Eat it, it's good for you. Don't put that in your mouth, you don't know where it's been. I don't care who started it. Get your hair out of your face. Don't think these eyes can't see you. If I didn't love you so much, I wouldn't care what you did. You'll have kids of your own one day. You call that music? Clean your plate, there are starving children. As long as you live in my house, we'll do it my way. Wait till your father gets home. If all your friends jumped off a cliff would you want to do it too? I don't care if everybody's doing it. Don't ever forget that mom loves you. You'll always be my Baby. ♥

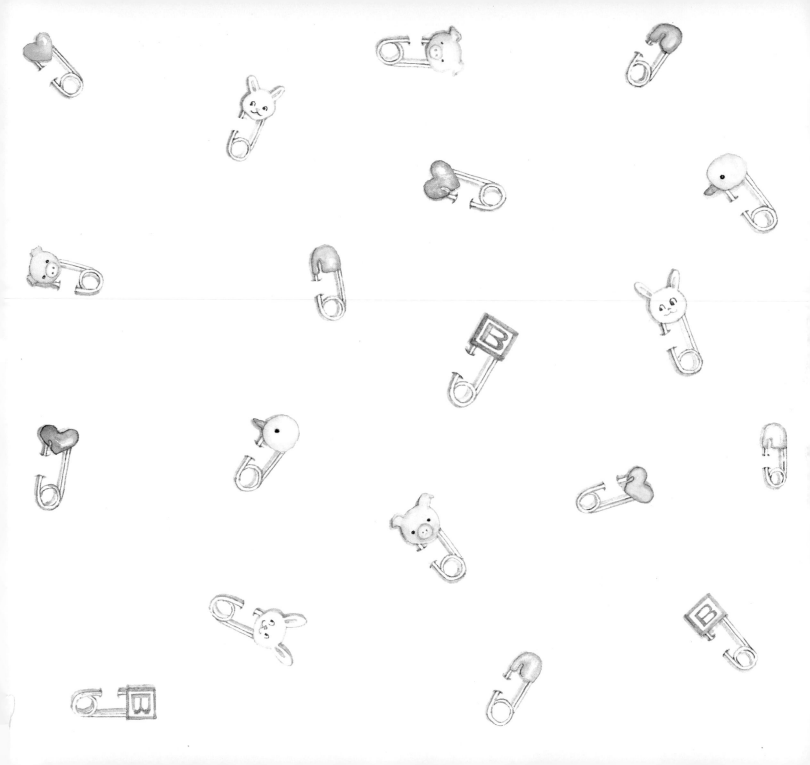

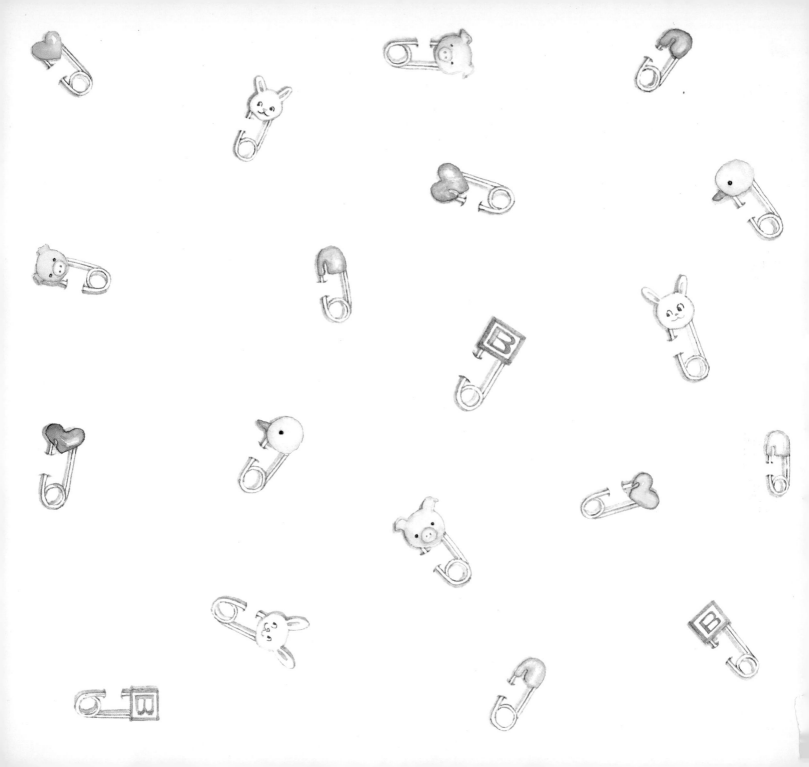